PIZZA

From Every Day to Gourmet

©2014 The Companion Group

Berkeley, California

800-521-0505

www.companion-group.com

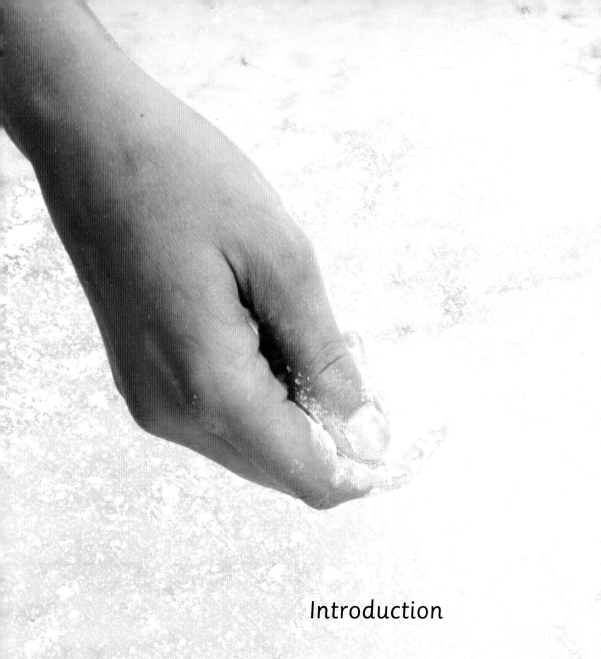

Introduction

Everyone loves pizza!

Pizza is one of those enduring things that follows you throughout your life. The sense memory of biting into a cheesy slice is as wonderful as an adult as it was when you were a kid. The comfortingly familiar sight, smell, and taste of hot pizza can bring up memories of family dinners when your parents relented and ordered delivery; those after-practice trips with the team to the local pizza joint; the birthday parties at a theme restaurant complete with a cartoon mascot serving up a slice. Later, those memories are of getting your first after-school job slinging pies at a chain franchise, or of relaxing with your friends, some pizza, and a couple of cold ones to watch the game.

More and more, those warm, welcome memories are being made right at home, as cooking pizza from scratch becomes more popular amongst the enthusiasts and economically-minded alike. Making pizza at home leaves you free to experiment, select the best ingredients, and save the money you'd have spent tipping your delivery guy. This book, written by pizza lovers for pizza lovers, will guide you through the at-home pizza making process, helping you to master your favorite food.

You don't need to be an expert at tossing dough high in the air in order to use this book; while it's fun to show off your pizzaiolo skills for your friends, we're more interested in eating pizza, not scraping it off the ceiling after a dough-spinning stunt goes awry. We've focused on finding a variety of different flavors to give you the complete pizza experience, from the traditional to the adventurous. You'll find dough recipes and techniques, suggestions for toppings, and creative, flavorful recipes. But we know we're not the final word on all things pizza. This book can be the start of not only the perfection of your homemade pie, but of pizza parties, family meals, and memories of good food and good fun.

No matter your pizza preference, we hope this book feeds your passion for pizza. Please share your pizza creations with us on Twitter, @_pizzacraft, and Facebook, www.facebook.com/pizzacraft.

Enjoy!

Table of Contents

Dough Recipes

The crust is literally the foundation of a great pizza. Thick or thin, crispy or chewy, it's more than just a delivery system for sauce, cheese, and toppings. Regional traditions play a role in the type of crust preferred (never stand in between a Chicagoan and a New Yorker arguing about whose pizza is better!), as well as personal taste. You'll need the right recipe and the right technique to achieve your ideal crust; the following recipes aim for a crisp and chewy thin crust, as well as deep dish and gluten-free alternatives.

The following pages include recipes for:

Thin crust pizza dough

Whole-grain wheat pizza dough

Cornmeal pizza dough

Deep-dish pizza dough

Gluten-free pizza dough

a. Dissolve yeast.

b. Yeast is ready when it has foamed up.

c. Combine yeast with other ingredients in a mixer with a dough hook.

d. Knead in mixer until dough comes together.

e. Knead dough by hand, then cover in an oiled bowl to allow it to rise.

Thin Crust Pizza Dough

There are as many pizza dough recipes out there as there are pizzerias, but after a lot of experimenting, we've found this recipe to be reliable, easy, and delicious. Neapolitan purists will point out that traditional dough does not contain olive oil, but its inclusion not only makes the raw dough easier to work with, but also adds a rich flavor and crisp texture.

Ingredients:

4 C.	all-purpose flour
2 ¼ tsp.	active dry yeast
1 Tbsp.	olive oil
1 ¾ C.	warm water (105° to 115°F or 40° to 45°C)
1 Tbsp.	kosher salt

Method:

Dissolve yeast in a small bowl of tepid water; whisk gently to fully incorporate the yeast. Let stand 5 to 10 minutes while yeast softens and starts to form a creamy foam.

Meanwhile, add the remaining ingredients to a large stand mixer bowl. Add the creamy yeast mixture and knead with the dough hook until the dough comes together, about 3 to 5 minutes. If the mixture is too dry add warm water 1 teaspoon at a time until dough comes together.

Transfer dough to a lightly floured surface and knead by hand until dough is soft and elastic, approximately 5 to 8 minutes. Place dough in an oiled bowl, cover dough with plastic wrap and place a dish towel over the bowl. Allow dough to rise at room temperature for one hour or until dough doubles in size.

Once the dough has doubled in size, turn it out onto a floured surface. Use a knife or dough scraper to cut dough into four equal sized pieces. Gently form each piece into a ball. Dust the dough balls with flour, cover with plastic wrap and let the dough balls rise for 20 minutes.

The dough is now ready for shaping. Follow the instructions in your recipe to finish the pizza.

This recipe yields enough dough for four 10-inch pizzas. If desired, dough can be cut in half for two 16-inch pizzas or cut in thirds for three 12-inch pizzas.

Whole Wheat Pizza Dough

Using whole wheat flour gives your dough more nutty flavor and breadlike texture, plus it retains fiber and nutrients that bleached, refined flours lack. You'll still need to use a little bit of all-purpose or bread flour in this recipe, as whole wheat flour is more fickle and resistant to stretching.

Ingredients:

2 ⅔ C.	all-purpose flour
1 ⅓ C.	whole-grain wheat flour
1 Tbsp.	sugar
2 ¾ tsp.	active dry yeast
¼ C.	olive oil
1 ¾ C.	warm water (105° to 115°F or 40° to 45°C)
1 ¼ tsp.	kosher salt

Method:

Dissolve yeast and sugar in a small bowl of tepid water; whisk gently to fully incorporate the yeast. Let stand 5 to 10 minutes while yeast softens and starts to form a creamy foam.

Meanwhile, add the remaining ingredients to a large stand mixer bowl. Add the creamy yeast mixture and knead with the dough hook until the dough comes together, about 3 to 5 minutes. If the mixture is too dry add warm water 1 teaspoon at a time until dough comes together.

Transfer dough to a lightly floured surface and knead by hand until dough is soft and elastic, approximately 5 to 8 minutes. Place dough in an oiled bowl, cover dough with plastic wrap and place a dish towel over the bowl. Allow dough to rise at room temperature for one hour or until dough doubles in size.

Once the dough has doubled in size, turn it out onto a floured surface. Use a knife or dough scraper to cut dough into four equal sized pieces. Gently form each piece into a ball. Dust the dough balls with flour, cover with plastic wrap and let the dough balls rise for 20 minutes.

The dough is now ready for shaping. Follow the instructions in your recipe to finish the pizza.

This recipe yields enough dough for four 10-inch pizzas. If desired, dough can be cut in half for two 16-inch pizzas or cut in thirds for three 12-inch pizzas.

Cornmeal Pizza Dough

You might need to sweep up after enjoying a slice of pizza with cornmeal crust, as it's notorious for leaving a dusting of cornmeal crumbs as you eat it. It's worth it for the added sweetness and texture that the cornmeal gives a pizza. Even if you're not making dough with cornmeal incorporated, you can still use a handful sprinkled on the outside of your dough to keep it from sticking to your peel or stone.

Ingredients:

3 ⅓ C.	all-purpose flour
⅔ C.	finely-ground cornmeal
1 Tbsp.	sugar
2 ¼ tsp.	active dry yeast
¼ C.	olive oil
1 ¾ C.	warm water (105° to 115°F or 40° to 45°C)
1 ¼ tsp.	kosher salt

Method:

Dissolve yeast and sugar in a small bowl of tepid water; whisk gently to fully incorporate the yeast. Let stand 5 to 10 minutes while yeast softens and starts to form a creamy foam.

Meanwhile, add the remaining ingredients to a large stand mixer bowl. Add the creamy yeast mixture and knead with the dough hook until the dough comes together, about 3 to 5 minutes. If the mixture is too dry add warm water 1 teaspoon at a time until dough comes together.

Transfer dough to a lightly floured surface and knead by hand until dough is soft and elastic, approximately 5 to 8 minutes. Place dough in an oiled bowl, cover dough with plastic wrap and place a dish towel over the bowl. Allow dough to rise at room temperature for one hour or until dough doubles in size.

Once the dough has doubled in size, turn it out onto a floured surface. Use a knife or dough scraper to cut dough into four equal sized pieces. Gently form each piece into a ball. Dust the dough balls with flour, cover with plastic wrap and let the dough balls rise for 20 minutes.

The dough is now ready for shaping. Follow the instructions in your recipe to finish the pizza.

This recipe yields enough dough for four 10-inch pizzas. If desired, dough can be cut in half for two 16-inch pizzas or cut in thirds for three 12-inch pizzas.

Deep Dish Pizza Dough

Buttery, flaky, and almost like pastry, deep dish pizza dough makes pan pizzas as close to "pie" as you can get without a fruity filling! This dough is pressed into the pan and then filled with your sauce, cheese, and toppings, so there's no need to worry about stretching and shaping it perfectly. Let your pan do the work, and enjoy the delicious results.

Ingredients:

2 ¼ tsp.	active dry yeast
1 ½ tsp.	white sugar
1 ⅛ C.	warm water (105° to 115°F or 40° to 45°C)
3 C.	all-purpose flour
½ C.	grape seed (or other neutral cooking oil)
1 ½ tsp.	kosher salt

Method:

Dissolve yeast and sugar in a small bowl of tepid water; whisk gently to fully incorporate the yeast. Let stand 5 to 10 minutes while yeast softens and starts to form a creamy foam.

Meanwhile, add the remaining ingredients to a large stand mixer bowl. Add the creamy yeast mixture and knead with the dough hook until the dough just comes together while remaining slightly sticky, about 2 to 3 minutes.

Form dough into a ball and transfer to a buttered bowl, turning dough to coat with butter. Cover dough with plastic wrap and drape a towel over the bowl. Allow the dough to rise at room temperature for 6 hours or until it has doubled in size.

After the dough has risen, punch it down in the bowl and let it rest covered for 15 minutes. Turn the dough out onto a lightly floured surface and roll it out to the desired circumference.

The dough is now ready for filling. Follow the instructions in your recipe to complete the pizza.

This recipe yields enough dough for one large 10 inch or two smaller, 6 inch round deep dish pizzas.

Gluten-free Pizza Dough

Avoiding gluten doesn't mean you cannot enjoy pizza! After all, what you really need is the right vehicle for a whole world of toppings out there. This gluten-free crust will have a different texture than conventional crust, but is an excellent foundation for a personalized pie. Pizza for all!

Ingredients:

2 ½ C.	gluten-free flour blend of your choice*
½ C.	flax seed meal
1 Tbsp.	xanthum gum
1 tsp.	kosher salt
6 tsp.	active dry yeast
2 Tbsp.	olive oil (plus extra for brushing)
1 Tbsp.	honey
1 ⅓ C.	warm water (105° to 115°F or 40° to 45°C)
1 tsp.	cider vinegar

Method:

In a small bowl, combine water, oil, honey, and vinegar. Add yeast and let bloom for 3 to 5 minutes.

Place dry ingredients in the bowl of your mixer. Add the yeast mixture and mix with your paddle attachment on medium for 3 to 5 minutes until the dough thickens. The result should be soft, pliable dough.

The dough is now ready for shaping. Follow the instructions in how to work with dough to create the crust.

This recipe yields enough dough for two 10-inch pizzas.

*We have had the best results with Pamela's® Gluten-Free Bread Mix. For a grain-free variation, replace the gluten-free flour blend with the following:

1 ½ C.	almond flour
1 C.	coconut flour
½ C.	flax meal
1 tsp.	kosher salt (in addition to above)

How to Work with Dough

Working with pizza dough is often the most intimidating part of making your own pizza from scratch. We've all seen the pros tossing and spinning dough high up into the air and catching it with ease. In home kitchens, such theatrics aren't necessary, though if you really want to practice, try tossing a damp dishtowel instead -- it's what pizzaiolos use for practice without wasting food!

Your goal is to shape the dough without over-handling and over-stretching the dough. It's easier than it sounds and as with all good things in life, practice makes perfect!

Thin Crust, Whole Wheat, or Cornmeal Dough

The most important part of the shaping process is making sure your dough has rested properly before attempting to toss or stretch it. After your dough has risen, divide it into portions if making more than one pizza. Gently form each portion into a ball by pulling and tucking the dough under. Place each dough ball onto a lightly floured surface, dust the dough balls with flour and cover with plastic wrap. Allow them to rest or at least 20 minutes. The dough is ready for shaping when it is warm to the touch and has risen again slightly.

To form your rested dough balls into a crust, work on a floured surface and flatten the dough into a disc. Apply pressure with your palms and fingers as you continue to work the dough into a larger disc.

Raise the dough up with both hands once the disc of dough reaches approximately six inches. Continuously rotate the dough through your hands, keeping them at the top while you let gravity evenly stretch the dough as it goes round and round. Grasp the dough just inside the edge to ensure a thin rim forms around the perimeter.

Drape the dough over the knuckles of both hands and continue to rotate the dough to further stretch it. Set the dough down for a moment and let it rest if it tears or begins to resist at all. Any small tears can easily be patched back together and will not adversely affect your finished pizza.

Once the dough reaches the desired diameter and thickness, move it to a floured pizza peel and form your crust into the desired shape. Proceed to top your crust with sauce and your desired toppings. Bake according to the directions in the recipe. Be sure to work quickly when topping your pizzas: the longer your dough sits on the peel, the more likely it is to stick.

Be patient when working with your dough. Achieving the perfect pizza crust can take some practice, but the journey is sure to be fun and delicious!

a

b

d

e

a. Divide your risen ball of dough into portions if making more than one pizza.

b–c. Gently knead each portion taking care not to eliminate air bubbles.

d. Form each dough portion into a ball.

e. Cover with plastic and allow them to rest for approximately 20 minutes.

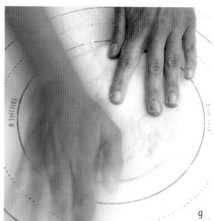

f

g

h

i

j

f–g. Place your rested dough ball back onto a floured surface and begin to flatten it into a six-inch disc.

h. Pick your disc of dough up and rotate it between your thumb and forefinger. Leave a ½-incih rim around the edge; allow gravity to stretch the dough as you rotate it.

i. Drape the dough over your fists and continue to rotate the dough as you stretch it to the desired circumference; if the dough resists, just set it down and let it rest for a moment.

j. The dough is now ready to be moved to your floured peel.

Deep Dish Dough

Not only is deep dish pizza completely satisfying to eat, it's also a great stepping off point for those who've never made or worked with raw dough before. You will find this dough to be extremely forgiving when rolling it out.

After your dough has risen, place it on a lightly floured surface. Divide the dough into portions if making more than one pizza.

Use a floured rolling pin to gently work the dough into a round shape, at least 2 inches wider on all sides of your pan, and approximately ¼ inch thick. Carefully transfer your dough into a pre-buttered deep-dish pizza pan. Press the dough onto the bottom and into the seams of the pan. Allow the dough to hang over the edge of the pan.

Next, add your deep dish fillings according to the recipe, then trim the excess dough using a sharp knife. Ideally, the dough and fillings will reach approximately 1 ½ to 2-inches up the side of the pan.

Bake the pizza according to the recipe, for approximately 45 minutes total or until the crust is golden brown and the cheese is golden bubbly.

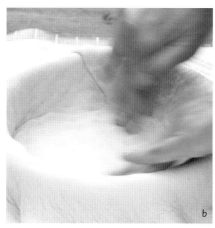

a. Roll out the dough in a circle shape.

b. Press into the pan, using your fingers to reach into the corners.

c. Add your filling.

d. Trim excess crust.

e. Ready to go into the oven.

a

b

c

d

e

a. Place dough onto parchment paper and form into a disc.

b. Cover with plastic wrap and shape into a 10 inch circle.

c. Brush lightly with olive oil.

d. Slide with parchment onto a pizza peel and transfer to the oven for pre-baking.

e. Remove from oven. Flip crust and add toppings to cooked side for final baking.

Gluten-Free Dough

Working with gluten-free dough is a little more like working with pie crust dough than working with conventional pizza dough, as it lacks the elasticity created by the presence of gluten. Rather than being stretched, this dough is intended to be hand pressed or rolled.

Preheat oven and pizza stone to 375°F (190°C). Place one portion of dough onto a lightly oiled piece of parchment paper. Form into a disc. Cover with a lightly oiled piece of plastic wrap. Use your hand or a rolling pin to press the dough into an even, 10-inch circle. Remove plastic wrap and brush the surface lightly with olive oil.

Slide pizza crust (on parchment paper) onto a pizza peel and transfer to your pre-heated pizza stone.

Bake for 20-25 minutes; remove crust from oven. Increase oven temperature to 400°F (204°C). Flip crust over on the parchement paper so that the browned side is facing up. Add sauce, cheese and toppings according to your recipe. Return pizza (on parchment paper) to oven and finish cooking another 8-10 minutes. The bottom of the crust will be nicely browned when the pizza is done cooking.

Note: This crust may be stored in the freezer for later use. After baking the first side, stop here. Let crust cool completely, seal in plastic wrap, and freeze. When you are ready to use the crust, let it first come to room temperature, then continue with the rest of the instructions to flip, add toppings, and bake.

Dough Add-ins

Pack your pizza with even more flavor by mixing herbs, spices, cheese, or other ingredients into your crust. These add-ins increase the complexity of your pizza's flavor, enhancing tastes already present in your sauce, cheese, and toppings. Be sure to account for the moisture content of your dough add-ins (if they're drier ingredients, you might need to add more water, and vice versa), and have fun experimenting!

Bacon – minced

Chocolate shards or shavings

Citrus zest

Fresh herbs, like basil, chives, thyme, or oregano

Garlic – minced, fresh or powdered, dried

Hard cheeses, like Parmesan or Pecorino

Nut meals – almond, pecan, or hazelnut

Olives – puréed

Spices, like cinnamon, cayenne, or cumin

Sundried tomato flakes

Sauce Recipes

It can be argued that it ain't a "real pizza" unless it has "red sauce." But the johnny-come-latelys of pesto and white sauces taste so good, who really cares? No matter the recipe, the goal of the sauce is to add moisture to your slice, and create a base upon which to build your cheese and toppings. In this book we offer suggestions for pairing sauce recipes with different doughs and topping combinations, but if you find that a new kind of sauce is calling to you, feel free to swap out the suggested sauce and substitute your own.

Red Sauce (Neapolitan-style)

Traditional Neapolitan sauce is all about the tomato. In fact, that's (almost) the only ingredient! With crushed, uncooked tomatoes and a pinch of salt, this sauce has the zest and juiciness of a tomato right off the vine. Even when garden-fresh tomatoes aren't available, the canned variety can give you similarly delicious results.

Ingredients:

1 can	whole, peeled tomatoes; 28-oz.
1 Tbsp.	kosher salt

Method:

Remove each tomato from the can and reserve 1 ½ cups of the puree. Cut the tomatoes in half, using your fingers, remove and discard the seeds. Remove any pieces of stem that may remain on the canned tomatoes.

Crush the tomatoes. You could do this by hand, in the food processor, or by running them through a food mill.

Transfer the crushed tomatoes to a bowl. Add the tomato purée and salt. Mix to combine.

This recipe yields approximately two cups of sauce.

Clockwise from top left: Red Sauce, Marinara, White Sauce, Pesto, Puttanesca

Marinara Sauce

Marinara sauce has more complex and mellow flavors than its Neapolitan sister. The ingredients are allowed to mingle and develop as they cook together, forming a richer, thicker pizza sauce.

Ingredients:

1 tsp.	olive oil
1	medium onion, small dice
1 Tbsp.	garlic, minced
1 Tbsp.	tomato paste
1 can	whole, peeled tomatoes; 28-oz.
½ tsp.	dried basil
1	Parmesan rind*

Method:

Heat a skillet over medium heat for one minute. Add the olive oil, followed by the diced onion and minced garlic. Sauté the mixture until the onion is translucent, approximately 6 minutes.

Add the tomato paste and sauté until the tomato paste begins to brown, approximately 1 to 2 minutes. Next, add the whole, peeled tomatoes and mash with a potato masher, leaving some chunks in the sauce. The tomatoes will continue to break down as the sauce cooks.

Add the dried basil and the Parmesan rind and bring to a boil. Turn the heat down and allow the sauce to simmer for 20 minutes.

Remove the Parmesan rind and season with salt and black pepper to taste.

This recipe yields approximately two cups of sauce.

*Instead of a Parmesan rind, add ¼ C. of finely grated Parmesan cheese to the finished sauce.

Puttanesca Sauce

Usually found on pasta, Puttanesca sauce has a bit of kick to it. The addition of red pepper adds spice, while anchovies, capers, and olives produce a strong umami flavor. This is marinara sauce taken to the next level!

Ingredients:

2 C.	Marinara sauce (recipe opposite page)
2	garlic cloves, minced
1 Tbsp.	anchovy paste (about 4 fillets)
1 Tbsp.	capers, chopped
½ C.	kalamata olive, minced
¼ tsp.	red pepper flakes

Method:

Combine the garlic, anchovy paste, capers, olives, and pepper flakes. Sauté in a sauce pan over low to medium-low heat for one minute until heated through.

Add the Marinara sauce. Bring to a boil, then simmer for 20 minutes.

Season with salt and pepper to taste.

This recipe yields approximately two cups of sauce.

Pesto Sauce

Bright green pesto sauce is a great alternative to the tomato-based "red" sauces. It captures the herbaceous flavor of leafy green basil and combines it with savory garlic, pine nuts, and Parmesan cheese. Use pesto as the base of your pizza, or brush some on top of a pizza with a red or white sauce base. This sauce can also be used on pasta, sandwiches, or as a dipping sauce for bread (or pizza crust!).

Ingredients:

4 C.	fresh basil leaves
2	garlic cloves
½ C.	toasted pine nuts
1 C.	Parmesan cheese
⅔ C.	extra virgin olive oil*
to taste	salt
to taste	black pepper, freshly ground

Method:

Combine basil, garlic, pine nuts, and oil in the bowl of your food processor or blender. Pulse the mixture until it is coarsely chopped.

Add the cheese and continue to pulse until the cheese is evenly incorporated. (Do not purée; you want to some texture to remain in the mixture.)

Transfer the mixture to a mixing bowl and season with salt and pepper to taste.

This recipe yields approximately two cups of sauce.

*This recipe contains less oil than most pesto recipes, but allow any excess oil to drain through a towel or coffee filter before adorning your pizza.

Pesto sauce can oxidize as it sits in your refrigerator. Make sure to give it a stir before using. You can blanch the basil leaves for 15-25 seconds to prevent them from oxidizing, but this step is not necessary. (It just adds to the visual appeal of the pesto.)

White Sauce

Using a rich, creamy white sauce creates a different pizza experience than its veggie- or herb-based counterparts. Tanginess and juiciness are replaced by smooth, subtle dairy-based flavors that complement more delicate and savory toppings such as mushrooms or ham. The garlic and Parmesan melted together with milk and butter make for a thick, pungent sauce that dresses up your average pizza.

Ingredients:

4 Tbsp.	butter
6 Tbsp.	all-purpose flour
2 C.	whole milk
⅛ tsp.	nutmeg, freshly grated

Method:

In a medium sauce pan, melt the butter over medium heat. Add the flour to the pan and use a whisk to make sure all of the flour is incorporated. Continue to cook and constantly stir the flour and butter, for approximately 2 minutes or until the mixture begins to take on a nutty aroma but has not changed in color.

Slowly whisk in the milk and bring to a boil. Lower the heat and simmer for approximately 20 minutes, stirring occasionally.

Remove from heat and stir in the freshly grated nutmeg. Season with salt and white pepper to taste.

This recipe yields approximately two cups of sauce.

Variations:

This recipe can be converted to gluten-free and/or dairy free. For a gluten-free version, replace the roux with about 1-2 Tbsp. of slurry. (To create slurry, mix cornstarch or potato starch with equal parts water or milk.) Add the slurry at the end of the cooking process to thicken the consistency of your sauce. For a dairy-free version, replace the milk with your choice of dairy-free milk such as almond milk or soy milk.

To make an alfredo-style sauce, gently sauté 5 cloves of minced garlic in the first step of the recipe. Follow the remainder of the recipe as written, adding 1 C. finely grated Parmesan cheese once the white sauce is removed from the heat for seasoning.

Your Own Toppings

The best thing about pizza is its versatility. You can top it with anything that will fit on top of your pizza -- and people often do. On one hand, you have traditional toppings like meat and veggies, but you can put literally any kind of food on your pie. Pizza-makers from other countries use this opportunity to make the pizza their own, adding toppings like curried lamb, seaweed, or escargot! If you have a favorite food (other than pizza, obviously), try adding little bits of it to your toppings. And if your second-favorite food happens to be chocolate cake, well, that's why we have recipes for dessert pizzas in this book!

Meats:

Canadian bacon

Carnitas

Chicken, grilled or roasted

Chorizo

Fish, smoked or canned

Ground beef

Ham

Linguica

Pancetta

Pepperoni

Salami

Italian sausage, spicy or sweet

Produce:

Broccoli or broccolini

Eggplant, roasted or fresh chopped

Garlic, fresh or roasted

Herbs, esp. basil, oregano, rosemary

Jalapeños, fresh or pickled

Kale

Mushrooms, button, crimini, wild

Olives, kalamata, green, black

Onions. fresh or caramelized

Pepperonccini

Peppers, sweet or hot, fresh, pickled, roasted

Pineapple, fresh

Potatoes, red or fingerling, roasted

Spinach, fresh or cooked

Tomatoes, fresh, roasted, or sundried

Cheeses:

4-cheese blend: Mozzarella, Asiago, Provalone, Romano

6-cheese blend: Mozzarella, smoked Provolone, Asiago, Romano, Parmesan, & Fontina

Cheddar

Chèvre (soft goat cheese)

Feta

Gorgonzola

Parmesan

Ricotta

Nuts:

Pecans, toasted or spiced

Walnuts, fresh or toasted

Almonds, sliced or slivered

Pignolias (pine nuts)

Recipes for Make-ahead Toppings

Some toppings suggested in this book take a little bit more prep than just chopping or shredding. These "make-ahead" toppings could practically be a meal on their own, but really shine when served on a pizza. Each recipe makes enough for one pizza, and should be multiplied if you are planning to serve several pies.

Braised Beets

Ingredients:

4	beets, medium size
¼ bottle	mild Cabernet wine
	water
½ tsp.	kosher salt

Method:

Wash beets thoroughly to remove excess dirt.

Place beets in a medium sized pot and fill with water to barely cover. Add red wine and salt. Turn flame on high and bring water/wine mixture to a boil.

Once water is boiling, reduce to a simmer. Simmer beets 30-40 minutes or until tender. To check tenderness, pierce beets with a wooden skewer. Skewer should be able to penetrate beet all the way to the center.

Cool beets and peel. Once beets are peeled, dice into small cubes or slice into ⅛ inch thick rounds.

Chocolate Ganache

Ingredients:

2 oz.	small shards of dark chocolate
¼ C.	hot, heavy cream

Method:

Bring the heavy cream to a simmer in a small pan.

Pour the heated cream over the chocolate pieces. Whisk continuously until the chocolate pieces have melted through. The chocolate and cream should marry together nicely, creating a homogenized consistency.

Carrot and Daikon Radish Slaw

Ingredients:

½ C.	water
¼ C.	sugar
	kosher salt, to taste
¼ C.	distilled white vinegar
½ C.	carrot, julienned
½ C.	daikon radish, julienned

Method:

In a small saucepan, combine the water, sugar, and vinegar and bring to a boil.

Transfer the vinegar mixture to a bowl and cool.

Add the carrot and daikon, mix well, and season to taste with salt. Set aside to marinate for 30 minutes or store in the refrigerator up to overnight.

Coconut Curried Chicken

Ingredients:

1	chicken breast, medium diced
2 stalks	lemongrass, outer husk removed and roughly chopped
2	shallots, roughly chopped
2	garlic cloves, smashed
1 inch	ginger, peeled and roughly chopped
1	jalapeño chili, seeded, stemmed, roughly chopped
2 Tbsp.	curry powder
1 can	coconut milk; 28-oz.
to taste	kosher or pickling salt

Method:

Place all ingredients (except the chicken) inside the jar of your blender. Puree for 2 minutes or until blended smooth.

Pour the curry marinade over the chicken and let sit between 2 and 4 hours.

Preheat oven to 350°F. Remove chicken from the marinade, place on a lightly oiled baking sheet, and bake for 10 to 12 minutes or until the chicken is thoroughly cooked.

Pickled Peppers

Ingredients:

1 ½ lbs.	chili peppers; your choice of hot and/or sweet
6 C.	vinegar
2 C.	water
5	garlic cloves, crushed
2 Tbsp.	kosher or pickling salt
2 Tbsp.	sugar

Method:

Wash peppers, then core and cut large peppers into strips. The small peppers may be left whole with two small slits in each pepper.

Combine vinegar, water, salt, and sugar. Bring to boil and reduce to simmer. Pour hot pickling solution over peppers. Allow to cool.

Peppers may be used right away or packed into sterilized jars for storage.

Piperade

Ingredients:

1	medium onion, small dice
1	medium red bell pepper, small diced
1	medium yellow bell pepper, small diced
4	Roma tomatoes, stemmed and small diced
2 oz.	ham, small diced

Method:

Sauté ham over high heat until it begins to brown. Remove from pan and set aside.

Sweat onion and bell pepper over low heat until they have softened. Add the tomato, turn the heat up, and cook over medium-high heat until the tomatoes have cooked through and most of the excess moisture has evaporated. Stir back in the ham.

Ratatouille

Ingredients:

¼ C.	bell pepper, thinly sliced
¼ C.	eggplant, thinly sliced
¼ C.	onion, thinly sliced
¼ C.	zucchini, thinly sliced
2 tsp.	garlic, roasted*
1 Tbsp.	tomato paste

Method:

Pre-heat your oven to 450°F (232°C). Toss the sliced zucchini, eggplant, and bell pepper in olive oil and season with salt and freshly ground black pepper. Spread them on a sheet pan lined with parchment paper and roast for 15 to 20 minutes until the vegetables are roasted through and have begun to caramelize.

*Place a head of garlic, with the top removed, on a piece of aluminum foil. Drizzle with olive oil, sprinkle with salt, then wrap tightly in the foil. Place in oven and bake in the oven 30 minutes or until the garlic is soft and caramelized.

Caramelize onions in a Dutch oven, sauté with some tomato paste, add the roasted vegetables and garlic along with canned diced peeled tomatoes. Bring to a simmer, adding a Parmesan rind if so desired, and stew together for about an hour. Season to taste and drain excess liquid.

Pizza Cooking Methods

Usually what comes to mind when you think of baking pizzas are those huge, brick, wood-fired ovens. While that's how the pros do it, it can be a little impractical to build one of those in your backyard (and if you live in an apartment, it'd probably violate all kinds of building codes!). Thankfully, we regular folk have many more options for baking our pizzas to crispy, golden perfection. Whether you're cooking it indoors or out on the grill, here are a few of the best ways to bake your pizzas.

Outdoor Oven:

Backyard ovens vary wildly in terms of size, cost, fuel, maintenance, and cooking procedures. You might have hand-built a rustic domed brick oven, or perhaps you've purchased a sleek metal appliance with state-of-the-art technology. Whichever one you have, your best bet is to follow the included instructions with your oven. That being said, here are some tips for outdoor oven cooking:

1. Always aim for the center of your oven's stone or hearth. If you're slightly off when you first transfer the raw pizza from the peel to the oven, wait 30 seconds before moving the pizza. The crust needs a few moments to cook just enough so that it doesn't fall apart upon moving.

2. Rotate your pizza at least once during cooking (sometimes even more, depending on your oven and your pizza) to ensure evenness.

3. Keep an eye on your pizza, and retrieve it from the oven as soon as it appears to be done: golden and crispy!

On the Grill:

This is a bit of a tricky technique, as you have to account for more inconsistent temperatures than you'd find in a traditional oven. Still, the ability to add a bit of smoky flavor – or just the novelty of making pizza on a grill instead of hot dogs -- makes the experience a rewarding one.

1. If you're using a stone, make sure that it is cordierite, not ceramic. Cordierite stones can withstand the intense heat of the grill without the risk of breaking when a cold, raw pizza is placed on top.

2. Allow your grill to preheat with direct heat for about 30 minutes, until it reaches 500°F (260°C).

3. When cooking, switch to indirect heat. Your pizza will probably take 15 to 20 minutes to bake fully, with golden toppings, bubbly cheese, and crisp crust.

The advantage of an outdoor pizza oven is that it can get hot enough to produce supremely crisp crusts.

Cordierite pizza stones can be use on both gas or charcoal grills.

Indoor Oven: Stone & Steel Method

Most people don't have special appliances just for pizza-making, and bake their homemade pies in a traditional kitchen oven. While most consumer ovens can't get as hot as a professional pizza oven, there are still ways to optimize your regular oven and turn it into a pizza-making machine.

1. First and foremost, you need a pizza stone or steel. Pizza stones, already mentioned in our grilling section, retain heat and bake your pizza's crust to crisp perfection. Stones come in ceramic and cordierite; cordierite stones absorb heat more effectively and are less prone to breaking, but ceramic stones are often less expensive.

2. Baking steels are similar in that they're large, flat platters that go in the oven and serve as the baking surface, but obviously they're made of steel instead of stone! Steels are a recent invention, but already pizza-makers prefer them to stones for their ability to conduct heat more efficiently while stabilizing at a lower temperature. Pizza cooked on steel achieves crisper, more evenly-cooked crust in less time.

3. If you can, using two stones, two steels, or a stone and a steel will help to recreate a pizza oven right in your own kitchen. Place one stone/steel on the bottom rack of your oven (if you're using both a stone and steel, you'll want the steel on the bottom). Then adjust your oven racks so that the one above the bottom is a few inches above it, and place your second stone/steel on top. Your raw pizza will go on top of the bottom stone/steel, while the second stone/steel creates a roof above it. That "roof" will radiate heat down onto the top of your pizza, cooking the toppings as the crust bakes underneath.

4. If your oven has a broiler in the top of the oven, you can try a different technique to bake your pizza. Adjust the racks so that the topmost rack is just underneath the broiler, and place your steel onto the rack. Turn your broiler on while your pizza is baking, and it will cook your toppings as the steel does its work.

5. No matter which of the above techniques you choose, pre-heating your oven is essential in order to get your stone or steel hot enough. In most ovens, it's best to turn it up as hot as it will go (for most ovens, between 500°- 600°F or 260°-315°C) and let it pre-heat for about an hour.

Pizza stones and steels can be used directly under the broiler in the oven.

Their heat retention makes them perfect for ensuring a crisp crust.

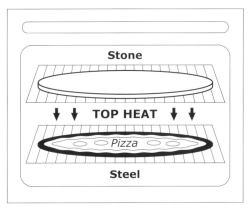

In combination, stones and steels will cook the toppings and crust evenly.

Equipment and Resources

In an ironic twist, the more advanced you become in making pizza at home, the fewer tools you'll need. Experienced pizzaiolos knead, stretch, and toss their dough with just their hands. But when you're just starting out, a few helpers like rolling pins and screens come in handy. Other tools like peels are essential no matter what your skill level; after all, you can't pull a pizza from a hot oven with bare hands!

Pizza Oven

Pizza ovens range from the high-tech to the low-tech, the expensive to the affordable, the huge and immobile to the light and portable. No matter what size, cost, or construction, the purpose of a pizza oven is to achieve the high heat needed to bake pizzas to a crunchy, chewy consistency. Traditionally wood-burning, there are now options for gas and electric ovens as well.

Pizza (or Baking) Stones

As discussed in "Cooking Methods," baking stones are flat tiles that serve as the cooking surface for your pizza, as opposed to a cookie sheet or pizza pan. Ceramic stones are a good economic choice for oven use only. Cordierite stones are mineral made, can absorb more heat, and are more durable for oven or grill use. All stones should be pre-heated before cooking, and cleaned once cool, with a brush.

Pizza Steel

A relative newcomer to the pizza scene, pizza steels are like stones in that they serve as a baking surface. However, the metal can radiate more heat than stone, and stabilizes at a lower temperature.

Pizza Peel

You've probably seen these, but not known the word for them. Pizza peels are those large, long-handled paddles used to transport pizza to and from the oven. They can be made of wood or metal, and come in a variety of different sizes and styles. They're usually solid, but some have perforations to prevent the pizza from sticking. Whether your peel has perforations or not, you should always dust it with flour or cornmeal before using it, to keep raw dough from sticking.

Infrared Instant-Read Thermometer

It can be difficult to tell exactly how hot your stone or steel is, so a infrared thermometer is handy when determining if your cooking surface is hot enough. Using laser technology, it bounces the light beam off of the cooking surface to read the temperature. These thermometers do not read ambient temperature.

Non-Stick Dough Mat
A dough mat not only serves as a great work surface, but many mats have measurements printed on them so that you can shape your dough to just the right size. As a bonus, putting flour on the mat and working your dough there makes for easy cleanup!

Dough Scraper
These broad, handled blades can scrape dough off of your work surface (especially handy if you're not using a mat), scoop up loose ingredients, or divide your dough into smaller portions.

Rolling Pin
If you're still starting out, you might need a little assistance in stretching out your dough. A traditional baker's rolling pin, either with handles or in one solid piece, helps to smoothly roll your dough to the correct thickness.

Pizza Screen
A pizza screen is metal pan constructed out of a mesh-like, perforated screen. This allows airflow around your pizza as it bakes, which is especially helpful if you don't have a stone or steel. A screen also helps novices who have yet to master using a peel, as the screen holds the raw pizza together and prevents it from sticking.

Deep Dish Pizza Pan
You can't make a deep dish pizza without one! Resembling more of a bread, cake, or pie pan, a deep-dish pizza pan has higher sides to keep in all those delicious toppings. A non-stick pan is preferable, and the best pans are constructed of anodized aluminum.

Pizza Cutter
As much as we'd like to eat a whole pie in one go, manners dictate that you slice up your pizza before you eat! There are many different kinds of cutters: a rolling cutter has a blade wheel that rotates and cuts as you roll it forward; a rocking cutter is a long, single curved blade that cuts across the diameter of your pizza in one motion; and, while less common, shears (scissors for cutting pizza) work well on thin crust pizzas.

Where to buy:
www.pizzacraft.com

Sur la table

Williams-Sonoma

www.amazon.com

While they're similar in shape, not all thin crusts are the same. As we covered in the dough recipes section, different ingredients and techniques can lead to unique tastes and textures. In this section, we've chosen topping combinations that we think work best with the prescribed crust. Some recipes are better suited for the sweetness of a cornmeal crust; others, the nuttiness of a whole wheat crust. If you're short on time, store-bought dough is a great shortcut.

Autumn Harvest

The warm orange and gold hues of this pizza echo the colors of changing autumn leaves. Fittingly, the ingredients bring out the flavors of a fall harvest, with butternut squash and sage. A bit of butter and Asiago cheese add salty contrast on a pizza that foregoes sauce in order to focus on these autumnal flavors.

Ingredients:

1 Tbsp.	butter
1 C.	butternut squash, medium dice
6 Tbsp.	Asiago cheese, coarsely grated
2 Tbsp.	sage, roughly chopped
1	cornmeal or other thin crust pizza dough round

Method:

Pre-heat your oven and pizza stone or steel to 550°F (287°C) for at least 20 minutes prior to baking. If using another method to bake your pizza, pre-heat accordingly.

Melt butter in a sauté pan over medium-high heat. Add the butternut squash to the pan and sauté until cooked through and lightly caramelized on the exterior. Transfer the cooked squash to a paper-towel lined baking sheet and season to taste with kosher salt and white pepper. Set aside.

Meanwhile, prepare your crust following the instructions in the how to work with dough section. Place your raw pizza crust on a floured pizza peel or pizza screen and sprinkle evenly with the butternut squash and Asiago cheese.

Bake for approximately 5 minutes, rotating the pizza halfway through. Remove the pizza from the oven when the crust is crisp and evenly browned. Allow the pizza to cool for one minute, then garnish with sage.

Forager's Delight

This pizza is so good it'll transport you to another plane of existence – while still using safe, totally legal mushrooms you can find at your grocery store. You can use farm-raised mushrooms like button mushrooms and criminis, or more hearty selections like foraged chanterelles, porcinis, and morels. This pizza is vegetarian as-is, but adding black forest ham is delicious!

Ingredients:

2 tsp.	olive oil
1 C.	mix of mushrooms, sliced ¼ -inch thick
2 tsp.	fresh thyme, finely chopped
¼ C.	white sauce (recipe page 23)
⅓ C.	mozzarella cheese, shredded
⅓ C.	fontina cheese, shredded
⅓ C.	asiago cheese, coarsely grated
1	thin crust pizza dough round of your choice

Method:

Pre-heat your oven and pizza stone or steel to 550°F (287°C) for at least 20 minutes prior to baking. If using another method to bake your pizza, pre-heat accordingly.

Meanwhile, heat a sauté pan over medium-high heat for 1 minute. Add the olive oil and mushrooms. Saute until the mushrooms are golden. Remove from heat and toss with 1 tsp. fresh chopped thyme, kosher salt and black pepper to taste. Set aside.

Prepare your crust following the instructions in the how to work with dough section. Place your raw pizza crust on a floured pizza peel or pizza screen. Use a spoon to evenly spread the white sauce around the dough. Sprinkle the dough and sauce with mozzarella, fontina and asiago cheese. Top with the cooked mushrooms and the remaining fresh chopped thyme.

Bake for approximately 5 minutes, rotating the pizza halfway through. Remove the pizza from the oven when the crust is crisp and evenly browned. Allow to cool for one minute before slicing to serve.

The Mediterranean

Take a culinary trip to the blue waters of the Mediterranean with this pesto pizza. The strong tastes of kalamata olives, goat cheese, and sun-dried tomatoes are dazzling on a bed of mellow mozzarella.

Ingredients:

¼ C.	pesto sauce (recipe page 22)
¾ C.	mozzerella cheese, shredded
⅓ C.	sundried tomato strips*
⅓ C.	kalamata olives, pitted and halved
⅓ C.	goat cheese
1	thin crust pizza dough round of your choice

Method:

Pre-heat your oven and pizza stone or steel to 550°F (287°C) for at least 20 minutes prior to baking. If using another method to bake your pizza, pre-heat accordingly.

Meanwhile, prepare your crust following the instructions in the how to work with dough section. Place your raw pizza crust on a floured pizza peel or pizza screen. Use a spoon to evenly spread the pesto sauce around the dough. Next, sprinkle with mozzerella cheese and garnish evenly with the sundried tomato strips and kalamata olives. Use two small spoons to top with dollops of goat cheese.

Bake for approximately 5 minutes, rotating the pizza halfway through. Remove the pizza from the oven when the crust is crisp and evenly browned. Allow the pizza to cool for one minute before slicing to serve.

*If not using oil-packed sundried tomatoes, rehydrate dried tomatoes before cutting into strips for this pizza.

Teriyaki Chicken

This tangy flavor combination is an eye-opener! Traditional chicken teriyaki ingredients, like pineapple, onion, and bell pepper are vibrant on top of this pizza, while marinated teriyaki chicken brings in the flavors

Ingredients:

¼ C.	red sauce (recipe page 19)
1 C.	mozzerella cheese, shredded
½ C.	red bell pepper, cut into 2-inch strips
6 Tbsp.	Teriyaki chicken breast or thigh meat, medium diced*
1 Tbsp.	pineapple, medium diced
1 Tbsp.	green onion, chopped for garnish
1	thin crust pizza dough round of your choice

Method:

Pre-heat your oven and pizza stone or steel to 550°F (287°C) for at least 20 minutes prior to baking. If using another method to bake your pizza, pre-heat accordingly.

Meanwhile, prepare your crust following the instructions in the how to work with dough section. Place your raw pizza crust on a floured pizza peel or pizza screen. Use a spoon to evenly spread the red sauce around the dough, within ½-inch of the edge. Next, sprinkle the mozzarella cheese evenly around the dough and sauce. Then, top with the red bell pepper, chicken and pineapple.

Bake for approximately 5 minutes, rotating the pizza halfway through. Remove the pizza from the oven when the crust is crisp and evenly browned. Allow the pizza to cool for one minute before garnishing with chopped green onion.

*To prepare Teriyaki chicken, simply marinate raw chicken breast or thighs in your favorite Teriyaki sauce overnight. Remove the chicken from the marinade (discard the sauce) and roast at 400°F (204°C) for approximately 30 minutes or until the internal temperature reaches 170°F (77°C). Cool thoroughly before chopping into a medium dice for this pizza.

Backyard Barbecue Chicken

Whether or not you're cooking this pizza on the grill, you can add that smoky barbecue flavor to your pie with this recipe. The chicken, onion, and barbecue sauce deliver notes of sweet, spicy, and tangy, while the smoked Gouda offers hearty, rich undertones. You can also swap the chicken for pork if that's your grilling go-to!

Ingredients:

¼ C.	barbecue sauce*
½ C.	mozzarella cheese, shredded
½ C.	smoked Gouda cheese, shredded
½ C.	cooked barbecue chicken breast or thigh meat, medium diced**
½ C.	red onion, thinly sliced
2 Tbsp.	fresh cilantro, chopped
1	thin crust pizza dough round of your choice

Method:

Pre-heat your oven and pizza stone or steel to 550°F (287°C) for at least 20 minutes prior to baking. If using another method to bake your pizza, pre-heat accordingly.

Meanwhile, prepare your crust following the instructions in the how to work with dough section. Place your raw pizza crust on a floured pizza peel or pizza screen. Use a spoon to evenly spread the barbecue sauce around the dough. Sprinkle the dough and sauce with both the mozzarella and smoked Gouda cheese. Top with the chicken and onion slices.

Bake for approximately 5 minutes, rotating the pizza halfway through. Remove the pizza from the oven when the crust is crisp and evenly browned. Allow to cool for one minute before garnishing with fresh chopped cilantro.

*A sweet and spicy barbecue sauce works best in this recipe. Our favorite is Steven Raichlen's Best of Barbecue™ Chipotle Molasses sauce.

*To prepare barbecued chicken, simply grill or cook chicken using your favorite method. Dice when cool enough to handle, and toss with barbecue sauce to coat.

Capra & Fiori

Inspired by the bounties of the Italian countryside, this pizza will delight the senses. Featuring a sophisticated palate of earthy and robust flavors, from the tang of fresh goat cheese to the delicate beauty of edible flowers, Capra & Fiora is truly a work of art.

Ingredients:

¼ C.	wine braised beets (recipe page 26)
1 ½ tsp.	fennel seeds, whole
1 ½ tsp.	cumin seeds, whole
½ C.	mozzarella, shredded
½ C.	Fontina, shredded
¼ C.	Chevre goat cheese
	wild arugula, small handful
	edible flower petals (ie: calendula, nasturtium, zucchini blossom)*
1 Tbsp.	extra virgin olive oil
1	thin crust pizza dough round of your choice

Method:

Pre-heat your oven and pizza stone or steel to 550°F (287°C) for at least 20 minutes prior to baking. If using another method to bake your pizza, pre-heat accordingly.

In a medium sized skillet, toast cumin and fennel seed approximately 3-5 minutes or until fragrant and browned. Transfer onto a plate to cool.

Blend shredded cheeses together. Set aside.

Meanwhile, prepare your crust following the instructions in the how to work with dough section. Place your raw pizza crust on a floured pizza peel or pizza screen. Brush crust lightly with extra virgin olive oil.

Sprinkle an even coating of cheese, then proceed to garnish evenly with the braised beets and half of the toasted cumin and fennel seed.

Bake for approximately 5 minutes, rotating the pizza halfway through. Remove the pizza from the oven 30 seconds before finished and add dollops of goat cheese. Finish pizza another 30 seconds in oven, remove and garnish with arugula, flower petals and remaining toasted fennel and cumin seeds. Drizzle lightly with extra virgin olive oil.

* Edible flower petals may be purchased pre-washed in a box in the produce section of the market.

Eat Your Veggies

Take advantage of your local farmer's market and pile on the fresh veggies! This pizza is loaded with vegetables, along with white garlic sauce and mozzarella. Perfect at the peak of summer when these veggies come ripe, this pie is fresh and colorful.

Ingredients:

¼ C.	white sauce, alfredo variation (recipe page 23)
1 C.	mozzarella cheese, shredded
1	heirloom tomato, sliced
¼ C.	bell pepper slices
¼ C.	red onion, thinly sliced
¼ C.	Niçoise olives
¼ C.	artichoke hearts
¼ C.	mushrooms, sliced
2	scallions, thinly sliced
1	thin crust pizza dough round of your choice

Method:

Pre-heat your oven and pizza stone or steel to 550°F (287°C) for at least 20 minutes prior to baking. If using another method to bake your pizza, pre-heat accordingly.

Meanwhile, prepare your crust following the instructions in the how to work with dough section. Place your raw pizza crust on a floured pizza peel or pizza screen. Use a spoon to evenly spread the alfredo sauce around the dough. Sprinkle the dough and sauce with the mozzarella cheese and top with the remaining ingredients.

Bake for approximately 5 minutes, rotating the pizza halfway through. Remove the pizza from the oven when the crust is crisp and the vegetables have developed some nice color. Allow to cool for one minute before slicing to serve.

Rosemary-Potato-Chicken

Tuck into some comfort food with this hearty recipe! The satisfaction of chicken and potatoes pairs with aromatic rosemary to create a gratifying meal.

Ingredients:

¼ C.	marinara sauce (recipe page 20)
1 C.	mozzarella cheese, shredded
1	chicken breast
½ C.	fingerling potato slices, 1/4-inch thick
2 Tbsp.	grape seed oil (or other neutral oil)
2 Tbsp.	fresh rosemary, finely chopped
1	whole wheat or other thin crust pizza dough round

Method:

Pre-heat your oven and pizza stone or steel to 550°F (287°C) for at least 20 minutes prior to baking. If using another method to bake your pizza, pre-heat accordingly.

Meanwhile, heat 1Tbsp. grape seed oil in a skillet over medium-high heat. Add the potato slices and fry for 1-2 minutes on each side until golden on the surface. Transfer cooked potato slices to drain on a paper towel; season with ½ Tbsp. fresh, chopped rosemary and kosher salt to taste. Set aside.

Use the same skillet to heat the remaining grape seed oil over medium heat. Chop the chicken breast into small chunks and transfer to the skillet. Season with kosher salt to taste and ½ Tbsp. of fresh, chopped rosemary. Continue to cook for approximately 3 minutes or until the chicken is cooked through. Set aside.

Now, prepare your crust following the instructions in the how to work with dough section. Place your raw pizza crust on a floured pizza peel or pizza screen. Use a spoon to evenly spread the marinara sauce around the dough. Sprinkle the dough and sauce with cheese. Top with the cooked chicken and potato slices.

Bake for approximately 5 minutes, rotating the pizza halfway through. Remove the pizza from the oven when the crust is crisp and evenly browned. Allow to cool for one minute before garnishing with the remaining fresh chopped rosemary.

El Greco

Bypass the Parthenon and go straight to the heart of Greece – its cuisine!
This pizza uses the quintessential Greek ingredient, olives, in addition to feta
cheese and spinach. If you're looking for a more traditional pizza, you can
add mozzarella cheese before the rest of your toppings.

Ingredients:

1 Tbsp.	olive oil
1	garlic clove, minced
2 C.	fresh spinach
¼ C.	red sauce (recipe page 19)
½ C.	mozzerella cheese, shredded
⅓ C.	feta cheese, crumbled
⅓ C.	kalamata olives, pitted and halved
1	thin crust pizza dough round of your choice

Method:

Pre-heat your oven and pizza stone or steel to 550°F (287°C) for at least 20
minutes prior to baking. If using another method to bake your pizza, pre-heat
accordingly.

Meanwhile, heat a sauté pan over medium-high heat for 1 minute. Next, add
the olive oil, minced garlic and fresh spinach. Use your hands to toss the
spinach around in the oil until it wilts enough to be managed with a spoon.
Turn off the heat and set aside.

Prepare your crust following the instructions in the how to work with dough
section. Place your raw pizza crust on a floured pizza peel or pizza screen.
Use a spoon to evenly spread the red sauce around the dough. Next, spread
the cooked spinach around the sauce; sprinkle evenly with the shredded
mozzarella and kalamata olives.

Bake for approximately 5 minutes, rotating the pizza halfway through. Remove
the pizza from the oven when the crust is crisp and evenly browned. Sprinkle
immediately with crumbled feta cheese. Allow to cool for one minute before
slicing to serve.

The "Banh Mi"

This pizza takes all the delicious fillings of a Banh Mi sandwich from out of the baguette and onto a pizza crust! Savory five-spice pork is topped with a fresh, crisp slaw and hit with a drizzle of hot Sriracha sauce. (Rooster sauce lovers might have their own definition of "drizzle," however...)

Ingredients:

2 oz.	ground pork
1 tsp.	five-spice seasoning
1 tsp.	grape seed oil (or other neutral flavored oil)
¼ C.	hoisin sauce
2 oz.	carrot and daikon slaw (recipe page 27)
	Sriracha sauce, optional
2 Tbsp.	fresh cilantro, roughly chopped
1	thin crust pizza dough round of your choice

Method:

Pre-heat your oven and pizza stone or steel to 550°F (287°C) for at least 20 minutes prior to baking. If using another method to bake your pizza, pre-heat accordingly.

Meanwhile, brown the ground pork in a skillet over medium heat. Add the five-spice seasoning and continue to cook until the pork is no longer pink. Remove from the heat and season with kosher salt and white pepper to taste. Set aside.

Prepare your crust following the instructions in the how to work with dough section. Place your raw pizza crust on a floured pizza peel or pizza screen. Brush crust lightly with oil.

Bake the pizza for approximately 3 minutes, rotating the pizza halfway through. Remove the pizza from the oven when the crust is crisp and evenly browned. Use a spoon to spread the hoisin sauce around the crust. Top with the cooked pork and return to the oven for 2 minutes or until the sauce begins to bubble.

Remove from the oven and allow to cool slightly before topping with the slaw and fresh chopped cilantro. Drizzle with Sriracha sauce to taste, if using.

A Light Lox Nosh

Think of this pizza as a lighter version of traditional cream cheese and lox on a bagel. Crème fraiche is spread over baked pizza crust and topped with smoked salmon, capers, and onions. You get a creamy, savory flavor that's great for breakfast.

Ingredients:

2 Tbsp.	fresh chives, finely chopped
¼ C.	crème fraiche
1 Tbsp.	capers (optional)
2 oz.	smoked salmon
1 tsp.	lemon zest
	olive oil
	coarse sea salt
1	thin crust pizza dough round of your choice

Method:

Pre-heat your oven and pizza stone or steel to 550°F (287°C) for at least 20 minutes prior to baking. If using another method to bake your pizza, pre-heat accordingly.

In a small bowl, combine half of the chives with the crème fraiche and set aside.

Next, heat 1 tsp. olive oil in a sauté pan over medium heat. Add the sliced red onion and sauté, stirring occasionally. Remove from heat once they begin to caramelize and set aside.

Prepare your crust following the instructions in the how to work with dough section. Place your raw pizza crust on a floured pizza peel or pizza screen. Brush with olive oil and sprinkle lightly with coarse sea salt.

Bake the pizza for approximately 3 minutes, rotating the pizza halfway through. Remove the pizza from the oven when the crust is crisp and evenly browned. Allow the crust to cool slightly, then top with the crème fraiche mixture, smoked salmon, red onions and lemon zest. Garnish with additional chives and capers, if desired.

The Peter Piper

Pick a peck of pickled peppers for this hot and sweet pizza! Both kinds of peppers are used, and your pizza's balance of spicy versus sweet can be tipped by using either hot or sweet Italian sausage. The use of Jack cheese creates a kicky Pepper Jack taste that's sure to pep you up!

Ingredients:

¼ C.	red sauce (recipe page 19)
1 C.	Monterey Jack cheese, shredded
4 oz.	hot or sweet Italian sausage
¼ C.	pickled hot or sweet peppers (recipe page 28)*
1	thin crust pizza dough round of your choice

Method:

Pre-heat your oven and pizza stone or steel to 550°F (287°C) for at least 20 minutes prior to baking. If using another method to bake your pizza, pre-heat accordingly.

In a small skillet over medium-high heat, brown the Italian sausage until cooked through. Set aside.

Meanwhile, prepare your crust following the instructions in the how to work with dough section. Place your raw pizza crust on a floured pizza peel or pizza screen. Use a spoon to evenly spread the red sauce around the dough. Sprinkle the dough and sauce with the Monterey Jack cheese. Top with cooked sausage crumbles and pickled peppers.

Bake for approximately 5 minutes, rotating the pizza halfway through. Remove the pizza from the oven when the crust is crisp and evenly browned. Allow to cool for one minute before slicing to serve.

* For store bought, look for Pappardelle peppers.

Rustic Ratatouille

The warm, savory sensations of ratatouille stew are served up on a slice of this delicious pizza. Normally a side dish, ratatouille is a traditional dish that originates from the south of France. In this pizza, the veggies are cooked separately and then stewed together, creating a rich and complex flavor.

Ingredients:

¼ C.	marinara sauce (recipe page 20)
1 C.	mozzarella cheese, shredded
½ C.	ratatouille (recipe page 29)
2 Tbsp.	Parmesan cheese, finely grated
2 Tbsp.	fresh basil, chopped
1	thin crust pizza dough round of your choice

Method:

Pre-heat your oven and pizza stone or steel to 550°F (287°C) for at least 20 minutes prior to baking. If using another method to bake your pizza, pre-heat accordingly.

Meanwhile, prepare your crust following the instructions in the how to work with dough section. Place your raw pizza crust on a floured pizza peel or pizza screen. Use a spoon to evenly spread the marinara sauce around the dough. Sprinkle the dough and sauce with the mozzarella cheese and top with small dollops of ratatouille.

Bake for approximately 5 minutes, rotating the pizza halfway through. Remove the pizza from the oven when the crust is crisp and evenly browned. Allow to cool for one minute before garnishing with Parmesan cheese and fresh, chopped basil.

Tastes of Thailand

No need to order takeout from Thai Palace – you've got all the flavors of Bangkok on one pie! Sweet coconut curried chicken is accented with peanut sauce and tamarind chutney for a refreshing meal that's a new take on the traditional.

Ingredients:

1 Tbsp.	neutral cooking oil
¼ C.	peanut sauce
3 oz.	coconut curried chicken, cooked and chopped (recipe page 27)
¼ C.	tamarind chutney
2 Tbsp.	fresh cilantro, stems removed
1	thin crust pizza dough round of your choice

Method:

Pre-heat your oven and pizza stone or steel to 550°F (287°C) for at least 20 minutes prior to baking. If using another method to bake your pizza, pre-heat accordingly.

Prepare your crust following the instructions in the how to work with dough section. Place your raw pizza crust on a floured pizza peel or pizza screen. Brush the dough generously with oil.

Spread the peanut sauce over the hot crust and top with chopped chicken.

Bake the pizza for approximately 3-5 minutes, rotating the pizza halfway through. Remove the pizza from the oven when the crust is crisp and evenly browned. Drizzle with the tamarind chutney and return to the oven for an additional minute, or until the sauce begins to bubble.

Remove the pizza from the oven and allow to cool before sprinkling with the fresh chopped cilantro. Serve with additional peanut sauce and tamarind chutney if desired.

Money Maker

This pizza is a sure bet. With sweet caramelized onions, meaty Italian sausage, tangy goat cheese, and a touch of oregano, this pizza is a winner! The only gamble you'll make is if you can get another slice before it disappears.

Ingredients:

1 tsp.	olive oil
1	clove garlic, minced
1 each	small red onion, thinly sliced
2 oz.	Italian sausage, casing removed
¼ C.	puttanesca sauce (recipe page 21)
½ C.	mozzarella cheese, shredded
2 oz.	goat cheese
1 Tbsp.	fresh oregano, finely chopped
1	thin crust pizza dough round of your choice

Method:

Pre-heat your oven and pizza stone or steel to 550°F (287°C) for at least 20 minutes prior to baking. If using another method to bake your pizza, pre-heat accordingly.

Meanwhile, heat 1 tsp. olive oil in a skillet over medium heat. Add the minced garlic and sliced red onion and sauté, stirring occasionally. Continue to cook until the onions begin to caramelize, about 12 minutes. Remove from heat and season with kosher salt and crushed black pepper to taste. Set aside.

Use the same skillet to brown the Italian sausage over medium heat until thoroughly cooked. Remove from heat and use a fork or spoon to crumble the sausage into small pieces. Set aside.

Now, prepare your crust following the instructions in the how to work with dough section. Place your raw pizza crust on a floured pizza peel or pizza screen. Use a spoon to evenly spread the puttanesca sauce around the dough. Sprinkle the dough and sauce with mozzarella cheese. Top with the cooked sausage, caramelized onions and small dollops of goat cheese.

Bake for approximately 5 minutes, rotating the pizza halfway through. Remove the pizza from the oven when the crust is crisp and evenly browned. Allow to cool for one minute before garnishing with fresh chopped oregano.

Latin Fiesta

Get a cerveza out of the cooler before taking a bite of this Latin-infused, flavorful pizza! This pie uses enchilada sauce instead of a red or white sauce to give it some heat. Pepper Jack cheese adds even more kick, and if you want to really spice things up, experiment with adding thinly sliced rounds of jalapeño.

Ingredients:

¼ C.	enchilada sauce
1 C.	Pepper Jack cheese, shredded
⅓ C.	carnitas (or grilled meat)*
¼ C.	tomato chunks
¼ C.	bell pepper slices
¼ C.	red onion, thinly sliced
2 Tbsp.	fresh cilantro, roughly chopped, optional
1	cornmeal thin crust pizza round

Method:

Pre-heat your oven and pizza stone or steel to 550°F (287°C) for at least 20 minutes prior to baking. If using another method to bake your pizza, pre-heat accordingly.

Meanwhile, prepare your crust following the instructions in the how to work with dough section. Place your raw pizza crust on a floured pizza peel or pizza screen. Use a spoon to evenly spread the enchilada sauce around the dough. Sprinkle the dough and sauce with the shredded Pepper Jack cheese. Use your fingers to spread the carnitas around the pizza. Top with tomato chunks, bell pepper and red onion slices.

Bake for approximately 5 minutes, rotating the pizza halfway through. Remove the pizza from the oven when the crust is crisp and evenly browned. Allow to cool for one minute before garnishing with fresh cilantro, if using.

*This is a great way to repurpose your bbq leftovers!

Flavor Flamenco

In order to keep this pizza true to its Iberian inspiration, it's essential to use real Spanish chorizo in this recipe. It's an aged, cured sausage seasoned heavily with paprika; Mexican chorizo is a raw pork sausage. Idiazabal cheese is a naturally smoky cheese from the Basque region of Spain (but we threw in some mozzarella to keep the cheese texture just right!).

Ingredients:

1 tsp.	olive oil
¼ bunch	kale, cut into 1-inch ribbons
¼ tsp.	smoked paprika
¼ C.	marinara sauce (recipe page 20)
½ C.	mozzarella cheese, shredded
½ C.	Idiazabel (or Manchengo) cheese, coarsely grated
2 oz.	Spanish chorizo, cut into ¼-inch rounds
1	thin crust pizza dough round of yoru choice

Method:

Pre-heat your oven and pizza stone or steel to 550°F (287°C) for at least 20 minutes prior to baking. If using another method to bake your pizza, pre-heat accordingly.

Meanwhile, heat 1 tsp. olive oil in a medium sauté pan over medium-high heat. Add the kale and sauté until it softens and begins to wilt, about 4 minutes. Remove from heat and season with smoked paprika, a few drops of sherry vinegar and salt to taste. Set aside.

Prepare your crust following the instructions in the how to work with dough section. Place your raw pizza crust on a floured pizza peel or pizza screen. Use a spoon to evenly spread the marinara sauce around the dough. Sprinkle the dough and sauce with both the shredded mozzarella and Idiazabel cheese. Top with the chorizo rounds and the cooked kale.

Bake for approximately 5 minutes, rotating the pizza halfway through. Remove the pizza from the oven when the crust is crisp and evenly browned. Allow to cool for one minute before slicing to serve.

Grilled Chicken Bianca

Gluten-free baking has come a long way in the past few years - serve this pizza as proof! Topped with the gooey goodness of garlicky, alfredo sauce, chunks of grilled chicken and just a touch of smoky bacon, each bite of this pizza is truly a gluten-free sensation!

Ingredients:

8	medium basil leaves, roughly chopped
1	chicken breast, grilled
1 C.	artichoke hearts, quartered
3	bacon strips
3 T.	white sauce, gluten-free & alfredo-style variations (receipe page 23)
1 C.	mozzarella cheese, grated
¼ C.	parmesean cheese, shaved
1 tsp.	olive oil
1	gluten-free pizza dough round (recipe page 15)

Method:

Preheat your oven and pizza stone to 375°F (190°C) for at least 20 minutes before baking. If using another method to bake your pizza, preheat accordingly.

Preheat grill for 15 minutes on high heat. Sear chicken on both sides, and turn flame down to medium. Cook 10-15 minutes per side or until internal temperature of 165°F (74°C) is reached. Remove chicken from grill and slice into strips.

Preheat a sauté pan over medium heat for one minute. Add the bacon and cook until brown and crispy. Remove bacon from pan and set aside.

Following the gluten-free dough method (page 15), form the dough into a 10 inch circle, prebake the first side for 20 minutes, and flip back onto the parchment paper. Increase oven temperature to 400°F (204°C).

Top pizza with cheese, basil, chicken, artichokes and bacon. Return pizza (on parchment paper) to the oven and finish cooking for another 5-7 minutes.

Remove the pizza from the oven and finish with freshly shaved parmesean and a healthy drizzle of extra virgin olive oil.

Ham n' Cheese

Rich and sharp, cheddar is the well-known companion of ingredients like ham (as simple-yet-satisfying sandwiches) and broccoli (as warm, ooey-gooey soup). Now, all three come together on one pizza! To make things a little lighter and more sophisticated, broccolini and Prosciutto are used in place of their heavier cousins.

Ingredients:

½ C.	broccolini
¼ C.	red sauce (recipe page 19)
½ C.	mozzarella cheese, shredded
½ C.	Cheddar cheese, shredded
2 oz.	prosciutto, roughly chopped
1	thin crust pizza dough round of your choice

Method:

Pre-heat your oven and pizza stone or steel to 550°F (287°C) for at least 20 minutes prior to baking. If using another method to bake your pizza, pre-heat accordingly.

Cut broccolini apart into thin spears. Bring a ½ C. of water to boil in a saucepan fitted with a steamer basket. Steam the broccolini for 2-3 minutes or until just tender and still vibrant green. Remove from heat and set aside.

Prepare your crust following the instructions in the how to work with dough section. Place your raw pizza crust on a floured pizza peel or pizza screen. Use a spoon to evenly spread the red sauce around the dough. Sprinkle the dough and sauce with both the shredded mozzarella and Cheddar cheese. Top with the chopped prosciutto and steamed broccolini.

Bake for approximately 5 minutes, rotating the pizza halfway through. Remove the pizza from the oven when the crust is crisp and evenly browned. Allow to cool for one minute.

The Green Gobblin'

Go green with this choloro-filled pizza recipe! You've got leafy, green spinach and soft, tangy artichoke hearts over a layer of herbaceous pesto sauce. Braising your artichoke hearts beforehand might be time-consuming, but it's definitely worth it; still, canned artichokes are delicious on this pizza too!

Ingredients:

1 tsp.	olive oil
2 C.	fresh baby spinach
¼ C.	pesto sauce (recipe page22)
½ C.	mozzarella cheese, shredded
½ C.	Asiago cheese, coarsely grated
¼ C.	medium onion, thinly sliced
¼ C.	artichoke hearts, quartered
1	thin crust pizza dough round of your choice

Method:

Pre-heat your oven and pizza stone or steel to 550°F (287°C) for at least 20 minutes prior to baking. If using another method to bake your pizza, pre-heat accordingly.

Meanwhile, heat a sauté pan over medium-high heat for 1 minute. Add the olive oil and fresh baby spinach, and cook until wilted. Remove from heat. Once cool, use your hands to squeeze excess liquid from the spinach and set aside on a paper towel.

Now, prepare your crust following the instructions in the how to work with dough section. Place your raw pizza crust on a floured pizza peel or pizza screen. Use a spoon to evenly spread the pesto sauce around the dough. Sprinkle the dough and sauce with mozzarella and Asiago cheese. Top with the cooked spinach, sliced onion and artichoke hearts.

Bake for approximately 5 minutes, rotating the pizza halfway through. Remove the pizza from the oven when the crust is crisp and evenly browned. Allow to cool for one minute before slicing to serve.

The Pie of La Mancha

Have a relaxing evening after spending the day tilting at windmills. Mix up a pitcher of sangria and indulge in this rich, sweet, and savory pizza! Savory Manchego cheese and Serrano ham contrast with the sweet, tangy piquillo peppers and even sweeter Membrillo quince paste.

Ingredients:

¼ C.	red sauce (recipe page 19)
½ C.	mozzarella cheese, shredded
½ C.	Manchengo cheese, coarsely grated
¼ C.	jarred piquillo peppers, drained and sliced
2 oz.	Seranno ham, thinly sliced
¼ C.	Membrillo paste*
1	thin crust pizza dough round of your choice

Method:

Pre-heat your oven and pizza stone or steel to 550°F (287°C) for at least 20 minutes prior to baking. If using another method to bake your pizza, pre-heat accordingly.

Prepare your crust following the instructions in the how to work with dough section. Place your raw pizza crust on a floured pizza peel or pizza screen. Use a spoon to evenly spread the red sauce around the dough. Sprinkle the mozzarella and Manchengo cheese around the sauce and dough. Top with the piquillo peppers and half of the sliced Serrano ham.

Bake for approximately 5 minutes, rotating the pizza halfway through. Remove the pizza from the oven when the crust is crisp and evenly browned. Sprinkle immediately with remaining ham and garnish with small dollops of Membrillo paste.

*Look for Membrillo (or quince) paste in the cheese section of specialty food stores.

The Hen House

Wake up your taste buds with a bite-sized version of a brunch favorite. The flavors of Eggs Benedict top this pizza, but in delicate, teensy pieces. Spears of asparagus are artfully chopped and cut on the bias, while tiny quail eggs take the place of chicken eggs. A sprinkling of lemon zest after cooking brings in the tang of Hollandaise sauce without all of the work!

Ingredients:

4 oz.	asparagus, cut into ½-inch pieces on the bias
¼ C.	red sauce (recipe page 19)
½ C.	mozzarella cheese, shredded
½ C.	pecorino cheese, coarsely grated
1 Tbsp.	capers
4	quail eggs
1 Tbsp.	lemon zest
1	thin crust pizza dough round of your choice

Method:

Pre-heat your oven and pizza stone or steel to 550°F (287°C) for at least 20 minutes prior to baking. If using another method to bake your pizza, pre-heat accordingly.

Bring a ½ C. of water to boil in a saucepan fitted with a steamer basket. Steam the asparagus for 2-3 minutes or until just tender and still vibrant green. Remove from heat and set aside.

Prepare your crust following the instructions in the how to work with dough section. Place your raw pizza crust on a floured pizza peel or pizza screen. Use a spoon to evenly spread the red sauce around the dough. Sprinkle the dough and sauce with mozzarella and pecorino cheese and top with blanched asparagus and chopped capers.

Place the pizza into the oven. Meanwhile, use a serrated paring knife to carefully open the top of the quail eggs. Leave the topped eggs sitting upright in the carton.

After about 4 minutes, take the pizza out of the oven and evenly disperse the quail eggs around the pizza, pouring from the cut end of each egg. Carefully return the pizza to the oven and continue to cook until the eggs have set.

Remove the pizza from the oven and allow to cool for one minute before garnishing with lemon zest.

The BLT

Like our Banh Mi recipe, this pizza is the adaptation of a classic sandwich onto a much larger (and rounder!) bread. Bacon and tomato top this pizza before it goes into the oven, while the arugula is added after baking so that it doesn't wilt. And yes, arugula isn't really lettuce, but who wants to eat a BAT?

Ingredients:

¼ C.	marinara sauce (recipe page 20)
1 C.	mozzarella cheese, shredded
2 oz.	bacon, cooked and roughly chopped
1	large fresh tomato, sliced
1 C.	fresh arugula
1 each	thin crust pizza dough round

Method:

Pre-heat your oven and pizza stone or steel to 550°F (287°C) for at least 20 minutes prior to baking. If using another method to bake your pizza, pre-heat accordingly.

Prepare your crust following the instructions in the how to work with dough section. Place your raw pizza crust on a floured pizza peel or pizza screen. Use a spoon to evenly spread the marinara sauce around the dough. Sprinkle the dough and sauce with mozzarella and top with chopped bacon and fresh tomato chunks.

Bake for approximately 5 minutes, rotating the pizza halfway through. While the pizza is baking, toss the fresh arugula with a drizzle of olive oil, black pepper and kosher salt to taste. Set aside.

Remove the pizza from the oven when the crust is crisp and evenly browned. Allow to cool for one minute before garnishing with the fresh arugula salad.

Breakfast Time

When this is what awaits you in the morning, you won't have to hit the snooze button! Your favorite breakfast foods come together perfectly on one pie, meaning every slice is full of eye-opening flavor. Serve with a glass of OJ and you'll be ready to start the day.

Ingredients:

2	strips of bacon
1	medium onion, sliced
2	fingerling potatoes
2	large eggs
½ C.	Asiago cheese, coarsely grated
½ C.	Fontina cheese, coarsely grated
1	thin crust pizza dough round

Method:

Cook the bacon in a sauté pan over low to medium-low heat until the fat has been rendered but the bacon is still soft and pliable. Allow the bacon to cool, then chope into small pieces and set aside. Reserve the bacon fat.

In the same skillet, heat the bacon fat over medium-high heat. Add the sliced onion and cook until deep golden brown. Remove from the pan and set aside.

Break the eggs into a small bowl and stir. Heat 1 tsp. of butter in a skillet and add the eggs, stirring them in the pan to scramble them as they cook. Continue to cook until the have just begun to set but are still slightly runny. Set aside.

Microwave the fingerling potatoes for 2 minutes or until just tender. Cut the potatoes into small rounds once they are cool enough to handle. Season with salt and pepper. Set aside.

Pre-heat your oven and pizza stone or steel to 550°F (287°C) for at least 20 minutes prior to baking. If using another method to bake your pizza, pre-heat accordingly.

Next, prepare your crust following the instructions in the how to work with dough section. Place your raw pizza crust on a floured pizza peel or pizza screen. Top the dough with scrambled eggs, grated cheeses, potato slices, chopped bacon and caramelized onions.

Bake for approximately 5 minutes, rotating the pizza halfway through. Remove the pizza from the oven when the crust is crisp and the cheese is melted. Allow to cool for one minute before slicing to serve.

Casablanca

Merguez sausage is a spicy lamb sausage popular in North Africa, especially Morocco. The white sauce, mozzarella, and chard help temper the heat, while its strong flavors transport you to the vibrant, diverse city that lends this pie its name. Here's looking at you, kid.

Ingredients:

1	garlic bulb
1 tsp.	olive oil
2 c.	chard greens, roughly chopped
¼ C.	white sauce (recipe page 23)
1 C.	mozzarella cheese, shredded
2 oz.	merguez sausage, casing removed
1	thin crust pizza dough round

Method:

Pre-heat the oven to 400°F.

Remove the top of the garlic bulb with a knife, revealing the cloves inside. Toss the bulb in oil and season with kosher salt and pepper to taste. Wrap in aluminum foil and roast for 50 minutes to one hour. Remove from the oven and cool completely. Once cool, squeeze the roasted garlic from the bulb and set aside.

Pre-heat your oven and pizza stone or steel to 550°F (287°C) for at least 20 minutes prior to baking. If using another method to bake your pizza, pre-heat accordingly.

Heat a skillet over medium-high heat for 1 minute. Add the olive oil and chopped chard greens and sauté until the greens are tender, approximately 3 minutes. Remove the skillet and set aside.

Use the same skillet to brown the merguez sausage over medium heat until thoroughly cooked. Remove from heat and use a fork or spoon to crumble the sausage into small pieces. Set aside.

Next, prepare your crust following the instructions in the how to work with dough section. Place your raw pizza crust on a floured pizza peel or pizza screen. Use a spoon to evenly spread the white sauce around the dough. Sprinkle the dough and sauce with the mozzarella cheese and top with cooked sausage, chard greens and roasted garlic.

Bake for approximately 5 minutes, rotating the pizza halfway through. Remove the pizza from the oven when the crust is crisp and evenly browned. Allow to cool for one minute before slicing to serve.

Bacon Breath

Admittedly, you'll need a mint after eating this pizza; its combination of garlic, bacon, chives, and three kinds of cheese is pungent! But for a slice of this tasty, salty, savory pie, it's more than worth it. Now, you might wonder why there are only two cheeses listed in this recipe – that's because the third cheese, Parmesan, is already incorporated into the sauce!

Ingredients:

¼ C.	white sauce (recipe page 23)
½ C.	mozzarella cheese, shredded
½ C.	Manchengo cheese, coarsely grated
3 oz.	bacon lardons
2 Tbsp.	chives, finely chopped
1	thin crust pizza dough round with bacon and chive add-ins

Method:

Pre-heat your oven and pizza stone or steel to 550°F (287°C) for at least 20 minutes prior to baking. If using another method to bake your pizza, pre-heat accordingly.

Heat a skillet over medium-low heat and brown the bacon lardons until some of the fat has rendered and the meat is slightly crispy. Remove from pan and set aside.

Next, prepare your crust following the instructions in the how to work with dough section. Place your raw pizza crust on a floured pizza peel or pizza screen. Use a spoon to evenly spread the white sauce around the dough. Sprinkle the dough and sauce with the mozzarella and Manchengo cheese; top with cooked bacon lardons.

Bake for approximately 5 minutes, rotating the pizza halfway through. Remove the pizza from the oven when the crust is crisp and evenly browned. Allow to cool for one minute before garnishing with chopped chives.

Pizzas Outside the Box

Our next few recipes are more like pizza's first cousins. They put a three-dimensional twist on your traditional round, flat pie (literally, in the rachetta's case!). You'll be surprised how a simple change of shape can affect your eating experience, so be sure to try them all, from pizza cones to calzones!

Stuffed Crust Pizza

There is no such thing as too much cheese. If you agree with that statement – if you're the kind of person who orders a four-cheese pizza with extra cheese and then STILL sprinkles on some grated Parmesan – this is the pizza for you. This recipe gives you the absolute easiest way to add cheese into your pie's crust, so you can indulge in your dairy delight in no time.

Ingredients:

¼ C.	red sauce (recipe page 19)
7	mozzarella sticks, cut into 1-inch pieces
1 C.	mozzarella cheese, shredded
1 Tbsp.	fresh oregano, coarsely chopped
1	thin crust pizza dough round of your choice

Method:

Pre-heat your oven and pizza stone or steel to 550°F (287°C) for at least 20 minutes prior to baking. If using another method to bake your pizza, pre-heat accordingly.

Prepare your crust following the instructions in the how to work with dough section. Place your raw pizza crust on a floured pizza peel or pizza screen. Place the one-inch pieces of mozzarella sticks edge-to edge around the perimeter of the crust, staying within one-inch from the edge of the crust. Roll the edge of the crust over the mozzarella stick pieces. Crimp the edge of the dough to seal the cheese into the crust.

Use a spoon to brush the crust with red sauce and sprinkle with shredded mozzarella cheese.

Bake for approximately 5 minutes, rotating the pizza halfway through. Remove the pizza from the oven when the crust is crisp and evenly browned. Allow to cool for one minute before garnishing with chopped oregano.

Four-Cheese Rachetta with Herbs

Pizza, anyone? The name "rachetta" is Italian for "racket," and true to the title, this pizza looks like you could pick it up and play a game of tennis. (We don't recommend it, though!) With a folded-over "handle," this pizza is part traditional pizza and part calzone, so both you and your doubles partner can have the meal you prefer!

Ingredients:

¼ C.	red sauce (recipe page 19
1	mozerella stick (cut to length of approx. ¼ of your pizza)
¼ C.	mozzarella cheese
¼ C.	asiago cheese
¼ C.	provalone cheese
¼ C.	Romano cheese
1 Tbsp.	fresh basil, finely chiffonaded
1 tsp.	fresh oregano or thyme, coarsely chopped
1	thin crust pizza round of your choice

Method:

Pre-heat your oven to 550°F (287°C). for 20 minutes with your pizza stone or steel inside or pre-heat according to instructions if using another method.

Place your pizza crust round on your floured pizza peel or pizza screen. Over one quarter of the pizza, place the cheese stick cheese where you envision the handle, leaving a ¾-inch border. Fold the dough over the cheese stick. Pinch to seal and create a flat handle. (You can also twist the dough around the cheese stick to achieve a fancier handle.)

Brush the rest of the rachetta with sauce, then evenly top with cheese.

Turn on your broiler and bake the rachetta for approximately 5 minutes or until done, carefully rotating halfway through.

Remove the Rachetta from the oven and garnish with the fresh herbs.

Ricotta and Piperade Calzone

If you want something more substantial than just a slice, a calzone is a hearty option. It's both filling and filled – in this case, it's stuffed with ricotta cheese and piperade. To keep things from getting soggy, the ricotta is drained before being folded inside, and sauce is served on the side for dipping.

Ingredients:

½ C.	ricotta cheese, well-drained
½ C.	mozzarella cheese, shredded
½ C.	piperade (recipe page 26)
	marinara sauce, to serve (recipe page 20)
1	thin crust pizza dough round of your choice

Method:

Pre-heat your oven and pizza stone or steel to 550°F (287°C) for at least 20 minutes prior to baking. If using another method to bake your pizza, pre-heat accordingly.

In a small mixing bowl, fold the shredded mozzarella and piperade into the ricotta. Set aside.

Prepare your crust following the instructions in the how to work with dough section. Place your raw pizza crust on a floured pizza peel or pizza screen. Distribute the ricotta mixture over one half of the pizza dough to within 1-inch of the edge. Fold the empty side over the filling to seal the edges. Use a fork to crimp the edge and to poke several air vents into the calzone.

Bake the calzone for 5 to 7 minutes, rotating halfway through. Remove the calzone from the oven once the crust is crisp and evenly browned. Allow the calzone to cool and rest for five minutes before serving with additional warm marinara sauce.

Deep Dish Pizzas

Get into the thick of it with these deep dish pies. Deep dish or "pan pizza" originated in Chicago – or at least, that's what the Windy City proudly proclaims! With buttery, flaky crusts and deep reservoirs of sauce, cheese, and toppings, these hearty pizzas are real heavyweights; one or two slices are enough to satisfy even the biggest appetite.

Meat Lovers

Declare your eternal devotion to your favorite toppings! This pie is stuffed with ground beef and salami, satisfying even the most enthusiastic carnivore. The savory meats combine with Italian seasoning and tons of cheese for a match made in heaven.

Ingredients:

1 Tbsp.	olive oil
⅔ lb.	ground beef
½ tsp.	Italian herb blend
½ tsp.	red pepper flakes
1 tsp.	garlic powder
1 tsp.	kosher salt
1 C.	marinara sauce (recipe page 20)
⅓ lb.	sliced salami, roughly chopped
5 slices	mozzarella cheese
1 ½ C.	mozzarella cheese, shredded
2 Tbsp.	Parmesan cheese, coarsely grated
1	deep dish pizza dough round (recipe page 6)

Method:

Preheat the oven to 375°F (190°C). Following the deep-dish pizza dough method (page 12), roll out and press the dough into a lightly buttered pan. Trim and discard any excess dough.

Meanwhile, heat the oil in a large skillet over medium heat. Add the ground beef and seasonings and cook until browned and cooked through. Season with salt and set aside to cool.

Combine the chopped salami, ½ cup of sauce, ¾ cup of shredded mozzarella and the cooked ground beef mixture in a bowl and set aside.

To assemble the pizza, place a layer of mozzarella cheese slices onto the dough. Spread the salami mixture over the cheese slices, filling the pan almost to the top of the crust.

Bake the pizza for 20 minutes. Remove from the oven and top with the remaining sauce, mozzarella and Parmesan cheese. Return the pizza to the oven and bake for an additional 25 minutes or until the crust is golden brown and the cheese is golden bubbly.

Allow the pizza to cool for 10 minutes before serving.

Roasted Vegetable with Pesto

This vegetarian deep-dish pie transforms a garden-fresh salad into a pizza masterpiece. By combining a variety of ripe veggies with herbaceous pesto sauce and lots of cheese, you get a hearty meal that's packed with flavor.

Ingredients:

1 tsp.	olive oil
2	medium onion, chopped
2	bell pepper, chopped
1½ C.	artichoke hearts, drained and quartered (or one 13.75 oz. can)
1 C.	cherry tomatoes, quartered
1 C.	kalamata olives, halved
5 slices	mozzarella cheese
1 ½ C.	mozzarella cheese, shredded
1 C.	pesto sauce (recipe page 22)
2 Tbsp.	Paremsan cheese, coarsely grated
1	deep dish pizza dough round (recipe page 6)

Method:

Preheat the oven to 400°F (204°C). Toss the onion and bell pepper with olive oil and some kosher salt to taste. Roast the vegetables in the oven until tender and beginning to caramelize, approximately 20 minutes. Remove from the oven and set aside. Reduce oven temperature to 375°F (190°C).

Following the deep-dish pizza dough method (page 12), roll out and press the dough into a lightly buttered pan. Trim and discard any excess dough.

Combine the roasted onion and bell peppers, artichoke hearts, cherry tomatoes, olives, ½ cup pesto sauce and ¾ cup shredded mozzarella cheese in a bowl. Set aside.

To assemble the pizza, place a layer of mozzarella cheese slices onto the dough. Spread the vegetable mixture over the cheese slices, filling the pan almost to the top of the crust.

Bake the pizza for 20 minutes. Remove from the oven and top with the remaining pesto sauces, mozzarella and Parmesan cheese. Return the pizza to the oven and bake for an additional 25 minutes or until the crust is golden brown and the cheese is golden bubbly.

Allow the pizza to cool for 10 minutes before serving.

Dessert Pizzas

As a kid, you might have been told that you couldn't eat dessert until you had finished your dinner. What about getting to have pizza after you've finished your pizza? These dessert pizzas can be served as a follow-up to a traditional savory pie, or alone as a special baked treat. With ingredients like chocolate, peanut butter, and fruit, they'll hit a sweet spot in your pizza palate.

Pears, Pecans, and Gorgonzola

Five simple ingredients come together in a gourmet pizza that's absolutely decadent. The visual appeal of this pizza will delight even the snobbiest of your foodie friends, while the taste will have everyone hooked. The sweetness of the honey and pear contrast the sharpness of the Gorgonzola, and the crunchy, nutty pecan halves add pleasing texture.

Ingredients:

½ C.	Fontina cheese, shredded
1	Bosque or D'Anjou pear, thinly sliced
¼ C.	Gorgonzola cheese crumbles
¼ C.	pecan halves, lightly toasted
1	thin crust pizza dough round of your choice
1 Tbsp.	wildflower honey

Method:

Pre-heat your oven and pizza stone or steel to 550°F (287°C) for at least 20 minutes prior to baking. If using another method to bake your pizza, pre-heat accordingly.

Prepare your crust following the instructions in the how to work with dough section. Place your raw pizza crust on a floured pizza peel or pizza screen. Sprinkle the dough and sauce with Fontina cheese and top with the pear slices, Gorgonzola and pecan halves.

Bake for approximately 5 minutes, rotating the pizza halfway through. Remove the pizza from the oven when the crust is crisp and evenly browned. Allow to cool for one minute before drizzling with honey.

Blood Orange Marmalade with Caramelized Fennel and Candied Ginger

This is a dessert for a more sophisticated palate. A layer of blood orange marmalade (or other marmalade, if you like) sets a sweet stage for the spark of candied ginger and caramelized fennel. Fennel goes with both savory and sweet pizzas, but here it really shines.

Ingredients:

2 Tbsp.	unsalted butter, melted
1 C.	fresh fennel, cut into ⅛-inch slices
1 tsp.	turbinado sugar
¼ C.	blood orange marmalade
2 Tbsp.	candied ginger, coarsely chopped
1	thin crust pizza dough round of your choice
	fennel fronds, for garnish

Method:

Pre-heat oven to 400°F (204°C). Toss the fennel with 1Tbsp. melted butter and roast until is soft and beginning to caramelize. Remove from the oven and toss with kosher salt to taste. Set aside.

Pre-heat your oven and pizza stone or steel to 550°F (287°C) for at least 20 minutes prior to baking. If using another method to bake your pizza, pre-heat accordingly.

Prepare your crust following the instructions in the how to work with dough section. Place your raw pizza crust on a floured pizza peel or pizza screen. Brush the dough with the remaining melted butter and sprinkle with the turbinado sugar.

Bake the pizza for approximately 2 minutes or until the sugar begins to caramelize. Remove the pizza from the oven and top with the blood orange marmalade, fennel and candied ginger. Return to the oven for another 3 minutes or until the crust is crisp and evenly browned. Watch the pizza carefully so that it does not burn.

Allow to cool for one minute. Add fennel fronds for garnish before slicing to serve.

PB & J

Make sure you have a big glass of milk to wash down this comforting classic!
Better known as the sandwich found in brown paper bags and school
cafeterias everywhere, this adaptation keeps that satisfying, sticky mix of
peanut butter and jam, while adding chopped roasted peanuts and fresh
berries to appeal to your "grown-up" side.

Ingredients:

2 Tbsp.	unsalted butter, melted
1 tsp.	turbinado sugar
⅓ C.	smooth peanut butter
¼ C.	strawberry jam
¼ C.	honey roasted peanuts, coarsely chopped
¼ C.	fresh berries
1	thin crust pizza dough round of your choice

Method:

Pre-heat your oven and pizza stone or steel to 550°F (287°C) for at least 20
minutes prior to baking. If using another method to bake your pizza, pre-heat
accordingly.

Spoon the strawberry jam into a squeeze bottle or piping bag and set aside.

Meanwhile, prepare your crust following the instructions in the how to work
with dough section. Place your raw pizza crust on a floured pizza peel or pizza
screen. Brush the dough with melted butter and sprinkle with the turbinado
sugar.

Bake the pizza for approximately 3 minutes or until the dough begins to brown
and the sugar begins to caramelize. Remove the pizza from the oven and top
with the peanut butter. Next, create a design over the top of the pizza using
the jam in the squeeze bottle or piping bag. Drag a toothpick through the jam
to enhance the design.

Return to the oven for 30 seconds to warm the peanut butter and jam.
Remove and sprinkle with chopped nuts and fresh berries to serve.

Chocolate Overload

The only thing better than a spoonful of Nutella is two spoonfuls of Nutella. The only thing better than two spoonfuls of Nutella is an entire pizza slathered with Nutella. Therefore, this pizza is the best dessert ever. Nutella is the perfect foundation for adding even more chocolate and hazelnut goodness. As Mae West said, "Too much of a good thing can be wonderful!".

Ingredients:

2 Tbsp.	unsalted butter, melted
1 tsp.	turbinado sugar
⅓ C.	Nutella or other hazelnut spread
¼ C.	chocolate ganache (recipe page 26)
¼ C.	white chocolate shards
¼ C.	toasted hazelnuts, roughly chopped
1	thin crust pizza round of your choice

Method:

Pre-heat your oven and pizza stone or steel to 550°F (287°C) for at least 20 minutes prior to baking. If using another method to bake your pizza, pre-heat accordingly.

Prepare your crust following the instructions in the how to work with dough section. Place your raw pizza crust on a floured pizza peel or pizza screen. Brush the dough with melted butter and sprinkle with the turbinado sugar.

Bake the pizza for approximately 3 minutes or until the dough begins to brown and the sugar begins to caramelize. Remove the pizza from the oven and spread with Nutella. Next, sprinkle with the white chocolate shards, chopped hazelnuts and drizzle with ganache.

Thanks to all of our contributors:
Wendy Boeger, Simone Chavoor, Sarah Goodwin,
Niki Gross, Danielle Peterson, Nick Wellhausen,
and to Chuck Adams for his patience.

Photographer: Sharon Kallenberger